Rosa Parks changed the
world in one day.

She was born Rosa Louise McCauley on February 4, 1913.

She grew up in Alabama. Alabama is a state in the South.

# Rosa Parks

### By Wil Mara

**Consultant**
Jeanne Clidas, Ph.D.
National Reading Consultant
and
Professor of Reading, SUNY Brockport

Children's Press ®
A Division of Scholastic Inc.
New York   Toronto   London   Auckland   Sydney
Mexico City   New Delhi   Hong Kong
Danbury, Connecticut

Designer: Herman Adler Design
Photo Researcher: Caroline Anderson
The photo on the cover shows Rosa Parks.

**Library of Congress Cataloging-in-Publication Data**

Mara, Wil.
  Rosa Parks / by Wil Mara.
    p. cm. – (Rookie biographies)
Includes index.
Summary: A simple introduction to the life of the woman whose actions
led to the desegregation of buses in Montgomery, Alabama, in the 1960s
and who was an important figure in the early days of the civil rights movement.
  ISBN 0-516-25876-1 (lib. bdg.)          0-516-27916-5 (pbk.)
  1. Parks, Rosa, 1913—Juvenile literature. 2. African American
women–Alabama–Montgomery–Biography–Juvenile literature. 3. African
Americans–Alabama–Montgomery–Biography–Juvenile literature. 4. Civil rights
workers–Alabama–Montgomery–Biography–Juvenile literature. 5. African
Americans–Civil rights–Alabama–Montgomery–History–20th century–Juvenile
literature. 6. Segregation in transportation–Alabama–Montgomery–History—
20th century–Juvenile literature. 7. Montgomery (Ala.) –Race relations–Juvenile
literature. 8. Montgomery (Ala.)–Biography–Juvenile literature. [1. Parks, Rosa,
1913- 2. Civil rights workers. 3. African Americans–Biography. 4.
Women–Biography.] I. Title. II. Series: Rookie biography
  F334.M753P38554 2003
  323'.092–dc21

                            2003003688

CHILDREN'S PRESS, and ROOKIE BIOGRAPHIES™, and associated
logos are trademarks and or registered trademarks of Scholastic Library
Publishing. SCHOLASTIC and associated logos are trademarks and or
registered trademarks of Scholastic Inc.
1 2 3 4 5 6 7 8 9 10 R 12 11 10 09 08 07 06 05 04 03

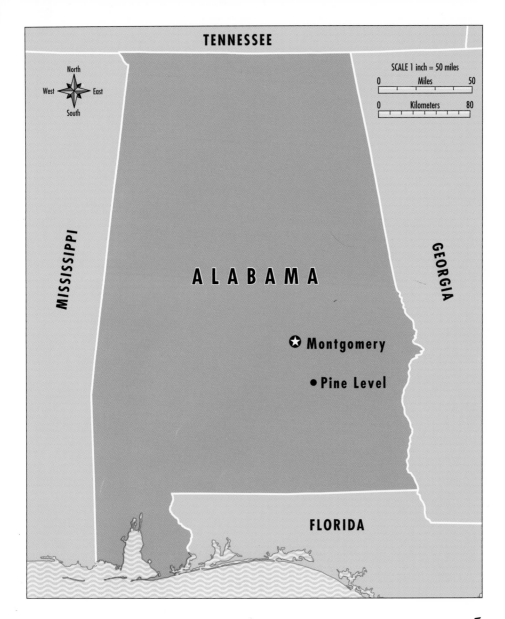

TENNESSEE

North

West ⬩ East

South

SCALE 1 inch = 50 miles

0      Miles      50

0      Kilometers      80

MISSISSIPPI

ALABAMA

GEORGIA

⭐ Montgomery

● Pine Level

FLORIDA

5

Rosa is an African American. When she was growing up, African Americans were called colored people.

The South was not a good place for African Americans to live. The South had laws that kept African Americans away from whites.

The laws said that African Americans could not go to the same schools as white people.

They could not eat in the same restaurants or drink from the same water fountains.

Rosa thought this was wrong.

On December 1, 1955, Rosa Parks was sitting on a bus. A white man got on. He wanted to sit in Rosa's seat.

The law said that African Americans must give up their seats to white people.

The bus driver told Rosa Parks to get up. She was tired of being treated this way. She said "no."

The police came and took her away.

14

Three days later, Rosa Parks went to court. She was fined 14 dollars. She didn't pay it.

African Americans were angry
about Rosa's arrest. They wanted
the laws changed.

On December 5, African
Americans held a boycott.
They said they would not ride
on any buses.

18

On that day, very few African Americans took buses. Many buses were empty.

# A meeting was held in a church in Montgomery, Alabama.

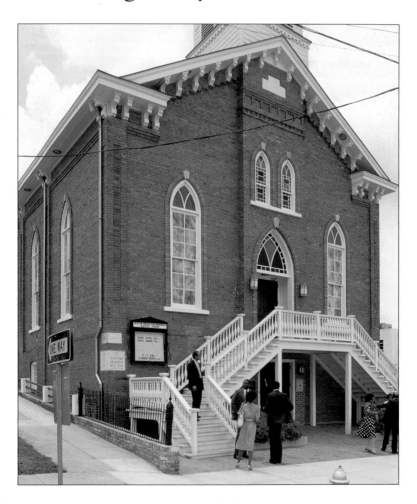

A minister told the people not to go back on the buses until the law was changed. His name was Martin Luther King Jr.

African Americans walked or rode in cars and taxis. They did not ride the buses in Montgomery for a year.

The buses stopped running because they didn't have enough people.

Finally, on November 13, 1956, the Supreme Court changed the law.

United States Supreme Court

Now African Americans could sit
wherever they wanted. They did
not have to give up their seats.

26

Rosa Parks kept fighting against the unfair treatment of African Americans.

She traveled to many places and talked to many people.

Rosa Parks made life better for all African Americans by just saying "no."

29

# Words You Know

African Americans

Alabama

arrest

boycott

Dr. Martin Luther King Jr.       Rosa Parks

Supreme Court

# Index

## About the Author

More than fifty published books bear Wil Mara's name. He has written both fiction and nonfiction, for both children and adults. He lives with his family in northern New Jersey.

## Photo Credits